Keyed In

7 KEYS TO TRANSFORM YOUR LIFE

CARLA C. HUGO

DEDICATION
To Tyler and Madison
You are my home.

TABLE OF CONTENTS

INTRODUCTION

I am so happy and grateful that you have joined me on this journey of self-discovery! As you read this book, know that I am your guide on the side as you unlock your inner power by becoming keyed in. You will successfully transform your life in the direction of your desires when you embrace the seven keys outlined in *Keyed In*. Throughout this book, you will see the phrase "keyed in." When you are keyed in, you are awake to your own thoughts and feelings. Rather than operate on auto-pilot or function from a reactive place, when you are keyed in, you will have clarity and confidence.

Each New Year, I attend a group guided meditation. This meditation is a way to release the old and make way for new and good to occur in the year ahead. The meditation leader conducts the guided tour that activates the imaginations of those in attendance. For the New Year kickoff, we are lead to an imaginary place where we have the opportunity to find our symbol for the year ahead. During one such guided meditation, the skeleton key, with its curvy, mysterious beauty, appeared in my imagination. The key became a token to notice during the new calendar year. When I spot a skeleton key, or the image of one, it is confirmation for me that I am in the right place at the right time. Since that time, skeleton keys have shown up in my life at just the right time. The skeleton key has been a meaningful symbol for me, and inspired the title of this book. It reminds me that new opportunities are on the horizon and that I have the ability to unlock my inner power. Being keyed in opens your personal portal to your inner awareness. Together we are going to venture into the place where your power resides. That place is in your thoughts and feelings. But without being aware of them, or without being keyed in, you will not achieve the greatness that awaits you. *Keyed In* is a means for me to show you a transformative power that resides within you.

So why are your thoughts and feelings so important? Your thoughts and feelings are so vital to your success in achieving your goals because they have a measurable energetic vibration. They pre-pave the way to your existence. According to Albert Einstein, all matter is energy, even the human form. Your thoughts and your feelings have resonance that seeks out a like vibration. Think of a tuning fork sending out a vibration to which voices and instruments align. This is how powerful your feelings are – they will align with the actual manifestation of events!

In seven chapters, I will describe for you the steps to unlock your inner power. Each chapter begins with an affirmation that I have created for you. Personally, when I read self-help and spiritual books, I break the rules. I open the book and begin reading wherever the page opens. Then I'll go back to the beginning and work my way through, from time to time reading random pages. I want you to have the same freedom with *Keyed In: 7 Keys to Transform Your Life*. While I wrote this book in a way that each chapter builds upon the next and references are made to previous steps, feel free to open to any page and read. I am confident that what you read will be exactly what you need to experience in that moment.

You will find that each chapter includes a segment called "Unlocked" where a guest writer shares a real-life story that exemplifies the chapter's key in creating transformation. Additionally, there is an Action Plan in each chapter. The Action Plan encourages you to take specific steps to implement the chapter's Key so that you receive the maximum benefit. Please take time to read the action steps. If you choose not to complete an Action Plan, you will still benefit by virtue of having read it. You will have a raised awareness of the action required to achieve the transformative key. With that awareness, you may just find that you are engaging in the essence of the steps in your own way, and will reap the benefits.

My hope is that you own the copy of the book you are holding, that you will break out a pen or pencil and write in your book, make notes, and complete your Action Plan.

I have been practicing as a Life Coach since 1997, and have expanded over the years to become certified in Emotional Freedom Techniques, ScreamFree Parenting, and Holistic Health Coaching. I am a graduate of the Institute for Integrative Nutrition, the world's largest nutrition school. Continuing education is a priority for me, so that I can be on the leading edge of new trends and offer the best, most comprehensive value to my coaching clients. I am sharing with you the steps that I use myself and impart to my cherished coaching clients. I am so grateful to them for collaborating with me, and for allowing me into their lives. And now, you have joined the party!

Thank you so much for being here now. You have my intentions for your highest good in hand.

Key 1

WHAT YOU THINK ABOUT,
YOU BRING ABOUT

My thoughts have power. I simply wave my mental magic wand
and choose a new thought. My thoughts pave the way for my
existence. I choose to make that paving process important and fun!

They happen all the time. They arrive with great speed. They come from many directions, sometimes with great focus and sometimes with none. These are your thoughts.

The first step to becoming keyed in and unlocking your transformative power is to raise your awareness to your thoughts. Take yourself off automatic pilot. Key in to your thoughts, because what you think about, you bring about. In the words of author and speaker Mike Dooley, your thoughts become things. Every experience in your life began with a thought. Ultimately, that thought became manifested. This book was a thought I had that has manifested into a reality. The computer on which I am typing was long ago an idea. Someone's idea for the computer became a reality. Your relationship with your mate was a thought. This thought was amplified by your desire to be in a relationship that aligned with your mate's desire to be in a relationship. Those thoughts and feelings paved the way for you to meet one another.

Since thoughts become things, it is of critical importance that you are keyed in. When you think a thought like, "I'm going to be late," you set yourself up to be late. Your actions will play out in such a way that you, in fact, become late. You have pre-paved the way for tardiness, and life will fulfill what you have set in motion. Your keys will be lost, traffic lights will be red, and parking spots will be in short supply. The Universe fails to hear "no," or words that negate truth. The Universe does not judge your thought or point you in the direction of something better. All of that is up to you. In other words, when you put your attention to "not being late" the Universe hears "...be late." The reason the Universe hears "be late" is that you have vividly imagined being late.

There is truth to the old saying "haste makes waste." But what brings on your haste? It's your thoughts. Fear and worry are often the corner stone of our thoughts. When you operate from a place of fear, you set yourself up for a negative experience. Fear exists in the *future*. It is very rarely in the present moment. Your thoughts are still manifesting, or coming into your reality, when they are negative. When you focus upon what you don't want to experience, you are putting your energy toward what you don't want. You may find that you are frequently visualizing exactly what you don't want.

Maybe it's that traffic jam or stumbling on your words on a job interview. Maybe you tell yourself you don't want to blow your diet today. "Don't wants" are powerful, and they send a magnified image of what you don't want to experience into the universe. Your emotions raise the vibration of your thoughts and make them even more powerful. Your "don't want" thoughts are magnified by fear. When you think of stumbling on your words in a job interview, and lacking the confidence to answer on-the-spot questions, are you experiencing that fear right now—or are you imagining it? Fear can be defined as the anticipation of future pain. Tune in and become aware when you feel the sensation of fear. Fear is in your thoughts, but how does it show up in your body? Do you feel tingling sensations, butterflies in your stomach, or sweaty palms? Pay attention to your thoughts and your bodily sensations around fear. When you know you are in a fear-state, you can take alternative action, rather than let fear guide you. When you are mentally in the present moment, it is extremely rare to be in a true state of fear.

When you notice your personal fear symptoms, take a moment to shift to an attitude of gratitude. Decide to be grateful for your fear. I know that sounds odd! But when you are keyed in, you are empowered to learn from your experiences. Go ahead and thank your fear for alerting you to the fact that you are focusing upon what you "don't want" to experience. Then, use this moment of gratitude as a hinge to turn your thoughts to what you *do want*. What you want to experience can be thought of in a way that is pure good and ease. Imagine walking out of your job interview feeling confident and excited about new opportunities to come. Imagine traffic flowing smoothly as you happily arrive at your destination on time. Put your thoughts toward imagining how you will feel when you have what you want. When you are keyed in, you have the ability to notice the thoughts that do not serve you. You can choose to think in a way that supports the outcome that you truly desire. Be aware and eliminate negative thoughts that surround your desired outcome.

AWARENESS IS KEY

I cannot emphasize awareness enough. When you approach your daily routine on autopilot, your expectations are for the same outcomes as yesterday. Your thought patterns fall into a rut and continue to bring about more of the same in your life. The key for you is to tune in and raise your awareness of your thoughts. It is helpful to really hear your thoughts. To do this, imagine there is a megaphone blasting your thoughts out into your surroundings. When I introduce this image to my coaching clients, they share that they would fear their children hearing their negative, self-deprecating thoughts. And these demeaning thoughts might also include foul language for emphatic purposes. So if your thoughts were magnified for the world to hear, would you even want to hear them? Would you want children to hear them? Your mate? Your boss? Allow the image of the megaphone to keep you keyed in to your awareness. At the same time, release judgment of yourself and your thoughts. Simply accept that this way of thinking no longer makes you feel good, and choose to reach for another thought. Routine, habitual thinking, and belief systems that no longer serve you dissolve under the bright light of awareness.

TIPS TO SHIFT YOUR THOUGHTS

Once you are aware of your thoughts, you then have the power to change them! The first step is to clear out the "don't want" aspect of your thought. Then re-state your thought so that it represents what you do want. With this clarity, you can magnify the energetic vibration of your thought by adding emotion to it. Remember how adding fear, a negative emotion, magnifies your negative thoughts? Choose positive emotions to magnify your desired thoughts. Begin to feel what it will be like to have the thing that you want. Adding emotion, which I like to call energy-in-motion, magnifies your thoughts and their ability to manifest on your behalf. The way fear is a magnifier that works against you, positive emotions are magnifiers that work with you to support you in achieving your desires.

Before long, you will have created new habits and a new comfort zone. As you continue to practice noticing your thoughts, and you bump into thoughts like, "I'm not good enough, I'm not thin enough, I'm not rich enough..." you will feel un-comfortable! Your new comfort zone will be in thinking thoughts that serve you. Choose thoughts that reflect where you are and where you want to be. You will notice your positive thoughts manifesting into your reality very quickly.

Another suggestion that I make to my clients and that I use my-self is that of a touchstone. A touchstone is an object that brings your awareness back into the present moment. You decide what your touchstone is. I enjoy using smooth pebbles and small seashells that I have collected from beautiful places as my touchstones. You may have a special charm or other object that works for you. Mix these up. When you feel your touchstone in your pocket or see it in your car, use it as a reminder to key in and decide if you are in the moment, in fear, in "don't want," in a place of ease, or in expectation. If you decide your thoughts are not in your best interest, be open to questioning what you actually want. Often, what you want is not simply the opposite of what you don't want. Key in and a surprising new idea may come to you.

According to Stephan Rechtschaffen, M.D., founder of the Omega Institute for Holistic Studies in New York, and author of *Time Shifting*, "If we push away the mundane, we push away the present. And when pushing away becomes our habitual pattern, we're likely to push away the extraordinary moments too, unable to fully savor them in our rush to 'get on.'" The lesson: Be present with the mundane.

Doing mundane chores is an exceptional opportunity to key in to your thoughts. When you wash a dish or fold a shirt, become aware! What are you thinking about? Where are your thoughts pointing you? If your thoughts were to manifest before you right now, how would you feel? Use the mental freedom of doing simple chores as an opportunity to stretch and grow your ability to think thoughts that further you along in life. Choose thoughts that represent gratitude for what you have and the desire for what you want.

How is what you are currently thinking serving you? Is it making you feel good about yourself and others? Does thinking this way make you feel comfortable? Are you willing to step out and create a brand-new comfort zone? Think thoughts of grandeur, self-love, deep appreciation, brilliant colors, light, and happiness. Key in and remember, what you think about, you bring about.

ACTION PLAN

Create a list of things you would like to think about. Remember the megaphone metaphor, and identify thoughts you want to shout out into the Universe. These are thoughts you feel fantastic about. Review your daily life and identify simple, new thought patterns that you can create. Here are some examples:

- Harmony in your love relationships
- Vibrant health
- Abundant success
- Grace
- Ease
- Prosperity in business

Identify and describe how you choose to think about each item listed below, with your keyed in awareness. Create your new thought patterns:

Today's Date: _____

My health _____

_____

My finances _____

_____

My opportunities for prosperity _____

_____

My personal growth _____

_____

My primary love relationship _____

_____

My relationship with my children _____

_____

My relationship with my parents _____

_____

My relationship with my colleagues _____

_____

My home _____

_____

My home life _____

_____

Travel _____

_____

Wealth accumulation _____

_____

Education _____

_____

Business ventures _____

_____

UNLOCKED: A TRUE STORY

I have been a "seeker" and an artist my whole life. With an undergraduate psychology degree and a graduate art degree, I was a high school art teacher for twenty years while married to my then-husband who I believed was "the real artist in the family." We shared a good life and happily raised two creative children together, now young adults. When the marriage ended (very sadly, for me), I had the chance to recreate myself in every way, growing more passionate on my spiritual search, developing as an artist, and eventually exhibiting and selling my own art work publicly in places I had never dreamed about.

By the beginning of this century (fun to say that!), I was a member of the Center for Spiritual Living Morristown, learning about the power we have in our own lives through the use of our minds. In 2003 I was introduced to the Law of Attraction as taught by Abraham-Hicks, a teaching that completely resonated with me in its overarching simplicity of focusing on what I wanted, and I steadfastly put it into practice.

With unbelievable ease, I lined up a one-person show at a large, local public art space in the county court administration building, a venue that could accommodate about sixty pieces of my work. At that time, I literally had four framed pieces, but the show was set for eighteen months away, so I needed to get busy!

I worked with Carla as a life coach and she helped guide me in my mental/spiritual practices as well as helped me create a time schedule, which I had to stick to, especially as the show date came closer.

I've always been partial to bold colors and strong linework, and I began painting stylized still lifes of things that attracted me—plates of blueberry pancakes and sausages, bowls of pears and papayas, arrangements of tulips and day lilies. I choose to paint only things that make people smile and feel good. I also included collages and photographs with inspirational text on them.

The name of my exhibit, and my art business, was born: "See the Good." I remind people that in this vibrational world, when you feel good by focusing on what makes you happy, you will bring more higher-vibration circumstances into your life.

In the weeks before I hung that inaugural show, I visited the space and pictured my work on the walls; I imagined people getting off the elevator and greeting me and my work with surprise and delight; I imagined selling a lot of my work and making good contacts.

The show came together with amazing ease and it was a huge success! It was the featured story in the arts section of a NJ newspaper. I sold many of my pieces and was offered exhibits in other venues. Since then, I've developed my website (www.seethegood.net), produced calendars of my inspirational work, had more than three dozen shows, and co-founded an artists' studio tour in the area. This is all within five years of my first one-person show, "See the Good." We can have and do and be whatever our hearts desire. We can use our minds and our power to bring about what we choose.

By Gail Mardfin - www.SeetheGood.net

Key 2

STRESS RELEASE AT YOUR FINGERTIPS

*Who can I be when I am carefree? Without worry about money,
unfinished chores, and family relationships, I am carefree. I visualize
my worries and fears floating away, as though wrapped in a just
blown bubble. I feel what it is like to be me when I am carefree.*

*A*wareness is the key to choosing what you think, so you can bring it about in your life. There are factors that undermine your ability to consciously choose your thoughts. For example, it is challenging to be keyed in when you are under stress. Regardless of stressors—whether it's finances, marriage, job, kids, or health—your mental clarity suffers because of your body's biochemistry. Two stress hormones in your body are cortisol and adrenaline. Although your lifestyle has evolved since the days of early man, your body's response to stress has changed very little.

Suppose you lived during the hunter-gatherer period. Imagine you were out hunting game when, suddenly, the game turned and started hunting you! When your brain receives a message that you are under threat, it signals your adrenal glands to release adrenaline. This is the immediate "rush" you feel when you are stressed, including an elevated heart and breathing rate, a burst of energy, and possibly sweaty palms. In a state of panic, you would run and find a place to hide or a tree to climb. Your body would be in flight-or-fight mode. Adrenaline is your body's immediate protection system. Cortisol is also released, and its job is to limit bodily functions that are not required to save your life from imminent danger. Cortisol shuts down systems like your immune, reproductive, and digestive systems. This "stress" hormone exists to support you in fleeing from the tiger that is threatening your life. In this mode of operation, your body is storing fat in fear that the next meal is not coming. You are spewing adrenaline and are operating at peak physical performance with reduced cognitive functioning.

Now think about being in a traffic jam and getting anxious about being late for a meeting. Although there is no wild beast chasing after you, your cognitive functioning is usurped by cortisol and adrenaline. Not only is your physical body suffering the consequences, your ability to remain keyed in is diminished.

STRESS INTERFERES WITH YOUR KEYED-IN THOUGHTS

There are many tools that I use and share to address stress release. For now, I am going to share how you can tap into your power to release stress, worry, and fear. In doing so, you will regain your ability to put your awareness on what you *want* to experience, instead of your suffering. Being under stress reduces your ability to bring about positive results in your life.

You may have an angry boss and your brain recognizes this stress and handles it in the same manner it would a life-threatening situation. These life-saving hormones alter your mood and your body systems for your benefit. When you are under sustained stress and continually feel under attack, your fight or flight reaction stays in the ON position, and your body processes become impaired. Stress contributes to reproductive challenges, weight gain, mood swings, and more negative consequences in your body.

Addressing and eliminating stress from your energy body will also contribute to mitigating these effects on your physical body. So what do I mean by *your energy body*? According to Albert Einstein, all matter is made of energy, including the human body. The ancient Chinese medical science of acupuncture indicates the body contains a series of invisible energy pathways. These pathways are called meridians. In this chapter, you will learn how to transform the flow of energy in your meridians. In 2006 I became a student of energy healing. I studied Emotional Freedom Techniques, or EFT, and received my certifications. EFT was founded by a gentleman by the name of Gary Craig. Gary is a Stanford engineer with a passion for helping war veterans who have suffered from post traumatic stress syndrome. Gary combined the fields of Thought Field Therapy and meridian therapies such as acupuncture, and created EFT. A common term for

EFT is tapping. He has been very generous to share this simple yet powerful healing technique.

Once you learn EFT, you are ready to tap into your power! EFT allows you clear access to your inner power—which is your keyed-in awareness—because it releases the stuck negative emotion from your body. EFT is an easy, effective leading-edge tool.

ONE OF MY PERSONAL EFT STORIES

Before I teach you how to apply EFT to release your stuck negative emotions or the pain of your physical ailments, I'd like to share the story of how EFT came into my life. Our daughter Madison was six years old at the time. She had suffered from chronic mucus production for five years. Madison was tested for allergies and had her adenoids x-rayed. These tests revealed no abnormalities, yet she would be up at night, coughing so hard that she would frequently vomit. My husband and I would take turns holding her upright overnight. We followed the doctor's orders which entailed medicating Madison with traditional, steroid-based decongestants, expectorants, and inhalers. Despite the medications, Madison's symptoms remained. There was so much vomit from coughing, that we disposed of the rug in our little girl's bedroom.

In the early Spring of 2006, I had reached the end of my proverbial rope with the spectacularly unsuccessful medical plan. I called a private meeting with our pediatrician in an effort to discuss and discover a new approach to her treatment. Our pediatrician suggested that we double the dose of Madison's medications! I left the office near tears, and was very determined to find another way. That evening, I searched the web with the term "healing night-time cough." The results came up with "EFT practitioner heals six year old son of night-time cough." I was astounded, especially since I was familiar with EFT and had already downloaded a book on the subject. I felt this was a huge synchronicity, because Madison was six years old as well. I couldn't wait to jump in and start tapping on Madi. I decided to train with professionals in California. One was a master practitioner who trained directly with Gary Craig. The other was a renowned acupuncturist who contributed her expertise on the meridian system to the training classes. I soon continued my training at The Clear Point Center in Connecticut and immediately began using the technique on Madison. I coupled EFT with the advice of a homeopathic practitioner, who suggested we remove dairy products from Madison's diet.

We embraced these two changes as a family, and to our amazement, Madison went off all medications and her symptoms disappeared—permanently! Madison learned to use EFT on herself, and would proudly come home from kindergarten to share that she had gone into the girls' room and had done some tapping. From my story, you see that EFT works on physical symptoms and you will learn it is equally effective on emotional concerns. And it is so easy, a child can do it. So, are you ready now?

TAP INTO YOUR POWER

When I lead my workshop on EFT, called Tap into Your Power, I use a balloon as a metaphor. Imagine a balloon that is just about blown up, but not completely taut. Then, picture yourself pushing a straight pin into the balloon. The balloon is flexible, and you can push the pin to a certain point without the balloon popping. Now imagine a nagging event going on in your life. Suppose you have stress about paying your bills. The balloon I described is a representation of your body, and the pin is the stress and worry you have around paying your bills. If you address the stress at the point I described, and use EFT to tap it away, the balloon is left unscathed. Suppose you choose the alternate path and continue stressing. Grab the straight pin and continue to push into the balloon. POP! Your imaginary balloon popping is symbolic of physical pain or illness manifesting in your body as a result of your unaddressed negative emotions.

It is commonly believed and agreed upon that stress leads to stomach ulcers. Yet there are often gaps in belief that other physical ailments are precipitated by emotional pain. I would ask you to lay aside your reservations and closely-held beliefs, and just come along with me for the ride. On a continual basis, our bodies are being bombarded with stress, fear, and feelings of being unworthy and unloved. Imagine all of those pins digging into you in varying degrees. When you implement a technique to address these stressors, you interrupt the transitional process of the emotional pain becoming physical. EFT is one tool that can be used to clear out this pain. To better understand how your meridian system works, I invite you to try this imagery, after you read about it.

Close your eyes and begin by engaging your mind with the image of a green garden hose. Imagine the hose is attached to a spigot with a red knob. Now turn the spigot to the left and watch the hose subtly inflate with water. Feel the coolness of the hose in your hands.

Next, bend down and fold the hose to form a kink. This garden hose that you have created in your mind's eye is symbolic of the meridians that run through your body. Energy naturally courses through your meridians, just as water flows through the hose. However, when you are experiencing a negative emotion that you are not addressing, it causes your energy to become blocked, just like the kink in the garden hose that you imagined. To un-kink your energy meridians, you can use EFT to overhaul your energy body. Now release your hold on the imaginary green garden hose and let the water flow freely.

Acupuncture addresses specific meridian points to heal particular bodily systems and functions. EFT, on the other hand, is an overhaul of the energy body and is a generalized approach. I will address ten tapping points. On each of these points, you will tap with your three middle fingers of both hands, on both sides of your body at the same time. When tapping, use moderate pressure. The diagram on the next page indicates the tapping points. The first point is the beginning eyebrow point. The second is the side of the eyes. The third point is under the eyes. The fourth point is under the nose. The fifth point is under the lip in the divot above your chin. The sixth point is the collar bone point. The seventh point is the side of the body on the ribs. The eighth point is on the front of your ribs and is known as the liver spot. The ninth point is on the soft side of both wrists. Rather than use your fingers to tap here, you can tap your wrists together. The tenth point is at the top of your head.

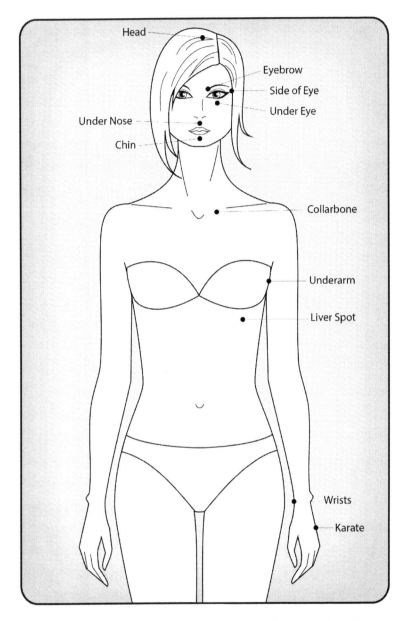

Head
Eyebrow
Side of Eye
Under Eye
Under Nose
Chin
Collarbone
Underarm
Liver Spot
Wrists
Karate

TAP ON BOTH SIDES OF YOUR BODY

If you have researched EFT or already know the technique, you may find that these tapping points are different from what you have learned. EFT is considered an art, which allows for varying applications. I mentioned that I studied EFT with a Master practitioner, an acupuncturist and continued my training at The Clear Point Center. My training coupled with my personal experience using and teaching EFT has confirmed my belief in the process. I have had tremendous success personally and professionally with EFT, and now it's your turn to experience the benefits. I am sharing my method to apply EFT. You are invited to view a demonstration video at keyedin.us/videos.

In an effort to measure your success with EFT, a scale was created called the Subjective Units of Distress Scale or SUDs for short. This scale uses the numbers zero through ten to measure your level of discomfort. Zero indicates that you have no pain or discomfort, and ten indicates extreme pain. It is important to assess your discomfort before you use EFT, so that you have a way of measuring your progress.

THE SET-UP

The first step to applying EFT is to do the set-up process. The purpose of the set-up is to bring your body's attention to the issue upon which you wish to work. For example, you may have a fear or worry that is in the future. You may not be presently experiencing the fear, but you become upset if you think about it. In EFT, the set-up is used to address concern about a future situation. Simply put, the set-up is intended to get you "upset" by bringing your attention to your challenge. To find the point upon which to tap when doing the

CARLA C. HUGO

set-up, imagine you are going to karate chop a block of wood. The place where your hand would hit the wood is the tapping point for the set-up, as indicated in the diagram. I prefer tapping both sides of my hands together at this point. Alternatively, you can use the fingertips of one hand to tap on the karate chop of your other hand. Again, engage both sides of your body. Just like your car going through a car wash, you want both sides cleaned at once.

The set-up step of tapping will bring your body's attention to the negative emotions you want to release. This is especially important if you are not experiencing the pain or discomfort right now. While tapping at the set-up point, there is a specific phrase for you to say. As you tap the karate chop point of your hands, say, "Even though I have this 'specific issue,' I deeply and completely love and accept myself." Repeat your set-up statement three consecutive times while at the same time, tapping the karate chop point. An example set-up statement is, "Even though I have this fear of flying, I deeply and completely love and accept myself." It is important to say these words *emphatically* and with feeling. You may have just experienced surprise at some aspects of EFT. First, the thought of saying that you deeply and completely love and accept yourself is likely an unusual sentiment! It's okay. Just go with it! Second, you may be wondering if focusing upon your problem or pain will make it worse. What I have learned is that we cannot fool our body. When we are in emotional pain, our meridian system is blocked and physical pain or illness will result. Addressing a problem with action within a system intended to relieve the problem will not draw more of the same to you.

When you have a pain or stress that you are experiencing in the moment, right now, it is not necessary to do the set-up, and you can proceed to the tapping as described next. The reason for this is that your body is already in tune to the issue you are experiencing emotionally. Think of the nervous response that occurs in your body when you are unprepared for an appointment or running late to work. The set-up is not needed because your body is experiencing your emotional discomfort and it does not need to be "upset."

TAP ON

Now, proceed to the tapping points as described above. At each point say a short version of your set up. The shortened version is called your reminder phrase. For example, "I'm scared to fly" is a reminder phrase that you can say at each point. Preferably, you will be able to get more specific. More specific examples might include: "I feel so trapped in this plane." "I am out of control." "I am entrusting my life to a stranger." "If there are storms, I will flip out!" Get creative and expressive. The more specific you are, the greater relief you will experience. Tap on each of the ten points while saying your reminder phrases. I recommend you tap approximately seven times on each point, which generally coordinates with the time it takes to say the reminder phrase. From time to time while you are tapping take a moment to pause and breathe. Take a deep inhale and a long slow exhale. Support the movement of energy through your body with your breath. Key in to your body. Notice if you experience tingling sensations, yawning, or even burping. These are common occurrences as energy is moved through your meridians. Remember, you are un-kinking the virtual hoses within you.

When you tap from the beginning eyebrow point to the top of your head, it is considered a round of tapping. After you complete one round of tapping, key in and check your SUDs. How has your number moved on the scale? Make note of this, and then continue tapping on the ten points, using your reminder phrases. After another round, you can return to the set-up step and say, "Even thought I still have some of this fear of flying, I deeply and completely love and accept myself." Or, you can say, "Even though my fear of flying is a five, I deeply and completely love and accept myself." This new set up creates a new level of awareness in your energy body. Then, as you do another round of tapping, your reminder phrase can reflect your lessened anxiety.

Your goal is to achieve a zero on the SUDs scale. However, getting your distress to register at a three or two is more likely, and is often enough for you to move on and feel tremendous relief. You will feel a weight lifted as your fear or anxiety has been acknowledged and reduced. There are many nuances with EFT and it is often helpful to have the perspective of a friend or a professional practitioner to guide you through the process. What I have shared with you are the steps to get started tapping and releasing your stuck negative energy. You can relax and know that while you may be able to have a better experience tapping with more practice or with coaching, you cannot do it wrong.

With EFT as a tool, you are prepared to address stress, fear, anxiety and pain. When you tap on your challenges, you minimize them as distractions and you allow in mental clarity. Your keyed-in awareness to your thoughts and feelings is your point of power. What you think about, you bring about and with a clean energy body, you regain control of your thoughts. Make tapping a go-to remedy, and you will find that you have expedited the manifestation of your desires.

ACTION PLAN

Identify an emotional issue or physical pain that you are currently experiencing that you would rate at a 7 or higher on the SUDs scale.

- What is your SUDs level?

- Have you addressed this issue before with a professional?

- How long have you been experiencing this issue?

- What types of treatments have you had for this issue, if any?

- What was going on in your life at the time when this issue first appeared?

How does having this pain serve you? By this I mean, although you would most likely rather be without this issue, is there a hidden benefit that keeps you holding on to it?

In answering these questions, you are having an experience similar to having a coach alongside you. Now begin with the set-up and proceed to a round of tapping. Remember to pause and breathe from time to time.

Clearing away your negative emotion and physical pain will enable you to remain keyed in to your thoughts and will empower you to choose the way you want to feel. Carefree!

UNLOCKED: A TRUE STORY

C: What life situation were you addressing when you decided to use the technique of EFT or tapping?

S: It was shortly after my old car died and my new car came into my life. Instead of being like a martyr of my circumstance, I purchased a car that was out of my league. I was feeling very heavy about my new car—it wasn't the right timing. I was upset with myself for getting a nice car instead of some beat up car. I didn't feel like I deserved a nice car! When I did a tapping session with you, that very day everything shifted about the car. Somehow, the things about the car that I had barely even noticed were things I wanted and now had manifested right before me in my driveway! Tapping through the points, I recognized that car was the manifestation of my own wants—not my "unwants." I have not had a problem paying for it. It has been safe and reliable and got me through sticky situations with weather. Now I feel proud of my new car and am so happy to have it! That was a huge shifting point for me with the tapping.

C: Wow, that is a huge shift and demonstrates how powerful our perceptions are. Your car is still the same car. Now that you have shifted from feelings of unworthiness to those of being grateful and empowered, you can feel great about your car. What else turned up for you when you tapped on this issue?

S: When I was younger, I didn't feel worthy. I always believed in hard work, and was stuck on the belief that good things come only when you torture yourself to get them. (Now that I mention it, this is something I can benefit from revisiting.) So as a result of the car breakthrough, I began tapping quite regularly on releasing my feelings about worthiness.

C: How much time do you spend on a daily, weekly, or monthly basis on the tapping process?

S: I don't call on it as much as I should. I did find myself tapping last week though. I didn't have time to go through the rounds and the reminder phrases, so what I did was tap my wrists while I was in a situation at work. This provided me with relief in the moment. I also have taken your suggestion and tap in the shower. I simply tap on the ten points and say phrases like: "I love and accept myself." "The day will bring what is meant to be." "All is in divine order."

C: Suppose someone has no idea what you are talking about! How would you describe this process in more detail?

S: There is a trust factor when you enter into that mindset of saying affirmations about yourself or your circumstances. I feel like when I put that out there energy-wise, I have a lot of faith that it returns. There is peace in that exercise for me. I believe that what I am affirming while tapping manifests.

C: If someone were to try tapping for the first time, do you have a tip for them?

S: From a logistic standpoint, it was hard for me to remember the points, so I created my own worksheet. That was really helpful to me. If it feels silly, do a little homework—do a little research. There is only positive stuff out there on it. It works. I had researched the film *Try It on Everything.* Bob Proctor shared it on the internet. I am a fan of Bob Proctor, and this gave it credence for me. I learned about it and then, as if on cue, a friend introduced me to you! The rest is history. The idea to try tapping on everything is very true. I need to do this more! That is one of the benefits of just talking about this today.

C: What kind of benefits have you seen in your business from doing this work? You've shared how you used tapping to come to a place of peace, ease, and gratitude around your car. What's next for you?

S: In business, there has been a palpable shift in my career momentum. I feel like I can really implement this in a larger way. I have spent less time practicing a number of good things that I was once so good about. I could probably tap on that, and release guilt for not doing these things! It's okay that I had a bump in the road, and it's okay to get back into tapping.

C: Remember the gifts in the bumps in the road. They are priceless. You are extremely busy juggling your personal, professional, family life. If you could use EFT to help your business, how would you do so?

S: I work in sales and it is stressful. I would first accept where I am and my insecurities. I would affirm my faith in the process and open up my energy flow in specific situations. I would affirm that I am meeting the right people and have the right inventory for them. I would tap on my ability to connect with those people and to build rapport. The potential is endless. Even when things are fabulous I could tap on making them more fabulous. It is definitely something I want to revisit and build back into my daily routine, not just in crisis mode. When I tap in the shower, I am cleansing and releasing. I am releasing self-doubt. I just had an "ah-ha" moment! When I tap in the shower about being behind and in a rush and then tap that it will all work out, that I love and accept myself even though I did not wake up on time, or left dishes un-done until the morning—I stay calm in the morning and don't scream at my children—even if they miss the bus! This is huge! Everyone wins!

C: So tapping is like a reset or a refresh.

S: Again, I'm calling on it in crisis mode, but want to call on it to make a good day even better. To reframe some of the hang-ups I have right now.

C: Any last thing you would want to share with our reader?

S: To just trust in the process. Have an open mind. And do it. Just do it! Some people may need some validation before they try it. Have faith that it will work.

C: Even though it can look and sound silly, and is likely outside of your comfort zone, let your guard down and be willing to step into it. Weird is okay, too!

Susannah Allen is a mother of two amazing children, a Realtor, and the CEO & CFO of her household. She holds personal growth and quality relationships paramount in all she does.

Notice how authentic Susannah is as she shares the benefits of EFT and her desire to use EFT more frequently in a variety of situations. Do not let perfectionism prevent you from stepping into this unique, powerful process.

Key 3

RELEASE RESISTANCE AND FILL YOUR OWN CUP

*Now is the time to examine my life. Am I awake to this
present moment? Have I released the "shoulds" and "could
haves"? Is my mindset one of appreciation? I have examined
myself and I choose consciously who I want to be.*

*G*et ready because Key 3 reveals how, when you transform yourself, the world around you responds in kind to support your
new outlook. This is so exciting, and I have created a simple process
where you use your keyed- in awareness to make it happen. Whether
your cup is half empty or half full, as long as you have exactly what
you want in your cup, it doesn't really matter. In other words, having your attention toward what you *do* want, even if only a small bit
of you is on board, you are empowered. In filling your own cup,
you release the need for striving and longing for what you want. You

replace feelings of lack with feelings of fulfillment. There is a big distinction between longing for something, which is the energy of lack, and acting as if you have that thing, which is the energy of abundance. In choosing abundant thoughts, and amplifying them with your awareness, you transform yourself.

How willing are you to experience life the easy way? This is a question I ask all new clients. Many people feel guilty when success is easily achieved, or they judge others harshly who seem to have it all with little effort. When you struggle to achieve something, does your success feel more valid than if the same result came effortlessly for you? If you answered yes, that feeling of validity comes from your belief in the outdated "no pain, no gain" strategy. I invite you to allow ease into your life. It's okay; you are not cheating on life's rules if success comes easily to you! When you push hard for something, as in "no pain, no gain," you will encounter resistance. What you push away pushes back. This is a natural law of the Universe.

RELEASE RESISTANCE

The phrase, "What you resist, persists" is attributed to Swiss psychologist Carl Jung. It implies that the more you resist a problem, the more it grows. By resisting, or pushing back against what you don't want, you energize that unwanted experience and attract more of the same. By resisting, you create a struggle for yourself. Mother Teresa is quoted as saying, "I was once asked why I don't participate in anti-war demonstrations. I said that I will never do that, but as soon as you have a pro-peace rally, I'll be there." Mother Teresa's words and deeds embody the idea of turning your attention from what you *don't* want and toward what you *do* want. In so doing, you will step into the flow of ease. How can you use Mother Teresa as a role model in your life? What are you resisting right now?

As you have now discovered, being keyed in is a state of being highly aware of your thoughts and feelings, being free of interfering stress, and being empowered to choose your thoughts. What you give your attention to grows. When you are resisting something, whether it is a change, a perceived conflict, or a forbidden food, you are adding energy to it and increasing its influence upon you. When you release your attention to the negative experience, it will naturally move on its way. Circumstances in your life will reflect your new point of view.

Wishing something away is a common thought process. When you wish for the absence of something, you are actually giving it attention and causing it to loom larger. For example, you may wish your hair was not turning gray. When wishing, it is likely you are counting all the gray hair on your head. Rather than wish, aim to surrender. In this case, surrender will bring you ease and peace. In my example, surrender could mean embracing your grays as a sign of your longevity and evolving beauty. When you shift away from wishful thoughts and surrender your resistance, you are able to make peace with what is.

Anger is another form resistance. Sometimes I will get angry with myself for something as common as catching a cold. I question, "Why me? I take great care of myself. How could I have been so weak as to be subject to this bug?" I am angry at my cough and feel sorry for myself. Guess what? I am setting myself up for more of the same. Struggle, wishing, and anger are all forms of resistance. Could I surrender and find the good in my cold? Yes, when I release my anger and resistance, then I can see how this cold provides me with a chance to slow down, get extra rest, and complete small tasks. I can key in and tap away issues that have been left unaddressed. Now it is your turn to ask yourself, how could having a problem, an ailment, or a troubled relationship serve me? What is the benefit? Flip a virtual switch and shift your attention away from this unwanted experience being a problem, and find a gift in it. When you focus upon the challenges and difficulties of life, your progress will be hampered and you will stay stuck in struggle. If you want it gone, you must let it go.

You can release resistance by surrendering, making peace with your situation as it is, or finding the benefit that arises from your challenge. Another option is to key in and raise your awareness to feelings of fear that arise from the situation you resist. Suppose you are putting off having a conversation with someone and are doing so because you have a fear of confrontation. The more you put off the conversation, the more the idea of it consumes you. What can you learn from your feelings of fear? Is your fear real in this moment? Is it a story you are telling yourself? You may find in answering these questions that you can either embrace or dissolve your fear. In either case, your state of struggle will be released. Replace your thoughts, feelings, and expectations with those of ease and doors will open for you as you pursue your goal. Surrender to what is. Release and find real *ease!*

Take a moment to notice what you are currently resisting. Identify a challenge you are facing and share it with your spouse or a friend. Then, describe what it is you really want to achieve. Next, identify what obstacles you feel are blocking your success. Tell your partner that you are looking to find opportunities for, rather than obstacles to, success. Allow your partner to be a sounding board for you, so you can release resistance and shift your focus to creating ease and opportunities.

SHIFTING GEARS

You must be keyed in to your thoughts and feelings to know both what you want and what opportunities are available to you. Think about traits you would *like to have*. Examples may include courage, strength, clarity, prosperity, and vibrant health. What portion of your time do you spend thinking about how you *want* to feel, rather than how you *actually* feel? It is easy to be highly tuned in to what is bothering you in the moment. Casual conversations are robust with "don't want" stories. Using a tool to subjectively measure and evaluate your feelings is helpful. I recommend a zero- to- ten scale to determine to what degree you are tuned in to your problems. Zero means you are at peace. Ten indicates you are consumed by worry, lack, and fear. Checking in by using this tool brings your keyed- in awareness to your thoughts and empowers you to take action. Use your score and begin to release worry and fear and create the mental space to ease back to zero.

FILL YOUR OWN CUP

Now that you know what you are resisting and are aware of the importance of releasing your resistance, it is time to fill your own cup with how you want to feel. This is the fun part! In the Action Plan at the end of this chapter, you will identify fifty situations, relationships, objects, or feelings that you want. Making this list will build a habitual thought pattern of keying in to what you want to experience. Like building your muscles by working out, you are creating muscle memory in your new thought patterns.

To implement the key of filling your own cup, choose one item that you would like to experience. For example, suppose having more money and the ease that accompanies it is on your list of fifty desires. Begin to fill your own cup starting today. To fill your cup, imagine an empty vase or vessel inside the core of your body and begin to fill it with feelings and images of financial abundance. Doing so will shift your energetic vibration from lack to that of comfortable wealth. Each time you encounter money use it as a reminder to visualize filling your cup. In your mind's eye fill the vessel with coins, cash and sparkling gems. Allow your pure desire for wealth and ease to become your prominent thought. (Money is not evil!)

Another way to fill your own cup is to imagine a thermometer with mercury rising as you notice and appreciate micro-moments of your desires. The tool I often choose when I visualize in this manner is a fundraising thermometer—the type of crafted thermometer used by volunteer organizations to track a fundraising goal. I imagine the rising red "mercury" as my virtual cup is being filled. Using this method and our example, the rising mercury indicates the growth of your financial prosperity. As money enters into your awareness, increase the mercury on your virtual thermometer. You may find a coin in a parking lot, have a check in the mailbox, or receive a coupon for a five dollar savings. Notice abundance in all forms and allow the mercury to rise. To amplify your prosperity consciousness, fill your cup with the abundance of nature. Depending upon the season, you may witness an abundance of green grass, autumn leaves, an endless ocean before you, or a glistening stream. Each of these images represents nature's abundance. Soak them in, internalize them, and become vibrant with abundance.

When you have even the smallest sense of feeling prosperous during the day, take notice.

As if you are putting coins into a piggy bank, fill yourself up with the feeling of prosperity. Be open up to this transformative process.

BE THE CHANGE

The act of filling your own cup may remind you of the popular phrase, "Be the change you wish to see in the world." This powerful statement is usually credited to Mahatma Gandhi. It is more likely a summary of his larger statement, "If we could change ourselves, the tendencies in the world would also change. As a man changes his own nature, so does the attitude of the world change towards him. ... We need not wait to see what others do." I love this! How empowering it is to know that in changing your thoughts, feelings, and actions, the world around you changes. You do not need to hand over your power and passively await change. When you fill your own cup, you become empowered. No longer are you waiting for others to provide you with your list of needs. Step into life as you want it to be, and make your desired experience your reality. By using your keyed-in awareness and visual imagination, you are empowered to become what it is you are wanting. As you transform from a state of lack to a state of being who you want to be, your life will respond to you in kind. Your spouse or mate, kids, boss, or colleagues will engage with you differently when you are filling your own cup. Situations will unfold for you in a more favorable and gracious way. Get ready to experience synchronicities, ease, and accommodations.

ACTION PLAN

Pick the visual that works for you. Choose from the empty vessel, the thermometer, or the piggy bank.

Raise your awareness as in Key 1. Decide what you would like to have more of in your life. Be vigilant about noticing abundance. As you receive a compliment, add it to your virtual vessel. As you receive money, add it to your vessel. As you receive kindness, add it to your vessel. Prosperity comes in so many forms. You may have an abundance of friends, cd's, blankets, or dandelions. Fill your virtual cup. You will *become* the thing that you felt you were lacking. This process will re-define who you are. In doing this exercise you shift your energetic vibration to that of a person who has abundance. Now that you are vibrating in alignment with your desires, the manifestation of your desired outcome is activated. Remember, what you think about, you bring about. When you become the change you desire, you are keyed in. Your reality will promptly align with your full cup and life will mirror your desire back to you.

My life is fulfilling when I have:

1._____

2._____

3._____

4._____

5._____

6. _____

7. _____

8. _____

9. _____

10. _____

11. _____

12. _____

13. _____

15. _____

16. _____

17. _____

18. _____

19. _____

20. _____

21. _____

22. _____

23. _____

24. _____

25. _____

26._____

27._____

28._____

29._____

30._____

31._____

32._____

33._____

34._____

35._____

36._____

37._____

38._____

39._____

40._____

41._____

42._____

43._____

44._____

45._____

46._____

47._____

48._____

49._____

50._____

UNLOCKED: A TRUE STORY

A professional writer for the past twenty-three years, I recently left a lucrative job at a local hospital foundation to follow my life-long dream. With Carla's coaching, I switched gears to embark on a new career path—working from home and writing fiction. In addition, I enrolled in a fiction writing workshop at The New School in New York City. Now, instead of accepting story assignments from others, my focus is self-driven and my writing is inspired by my imagination.

At first, the switch proved difficult for me. A trained reporter, I was used to following the facts and writing the truth. With fiction, I could make anything up and the only limitations came from my own creativity. A whole new universe was before me. There was no end to what I could produce. Or, in my case, no beginning.

I've always been a perfectionist, and as a writer, this can be deadly. The risk is censoring oneself before placing anything on the page. With Carla's gentle coaching, I've tried to put aside the notion that my first attempts should be perfect. Good writing, after all, comes from rewriting. But my self-criticism and my fear of failure dogged me in my new fiction writing pursuits.

Working with Carla, I learned to create a plan to support my writing and to nurture myself in the process. For example, instead of being rigid and setting aside a full day to write, Carla suggested I commit to short blocks of time, broken up by rewarding breaks, such as running or gardening. Where I had been reluctant to sit down and start writing – dreading the eight hours that loomed massively before me – I now had the freedom to sit and write for 45 minutes or an hour.

What I discovered was that once I started, I often found my groove and kept going long after the allotted time. And while the breaks nourished me, they also let my mind disengage. So many times, that illusive piece of my story I was puzzling over would come to me as I enjoyed the fresh air, one foot falling in front of the other as I jogged.

In dealing with my perfectionism, Carla would coax; "Just do it!" Just sit down and write. "Try something," she'd tell me. "And if it doesn't work, try again." So simple, yet such sage advice.

Once, when I was stuck on my plot and not sure how to proceed, Carla proposed using one of my strengths to assist me. As a writer, one of my strong points has always been my interviewing skills. "Why not sit down with your character and interview them?" she mused. Find out his favorite color, his dreams, the song that moves him to tears. This technique has helped me flesh out my characters and add depth to my stories.

Another of Carla's suggestions that proved helpful was for me to plan my day and block out when I would commit to writing. Schedule it. Be accountable. Respect my time. As a mother of two boys, I devote much of my time to my family. Putting my own writing high on my to-do list proved difficult. But I did it.

Other tools that Carla shared with me are affirmation and visualization. On my bulletin board above my desk, nestled among my happy family photos, I have two quotes: "Write Your Book" and "This Year You Write Your Novel." These two blurbs nudge me forward and remind me of my goal when my mind drifts.

Similarly, Carla has taught me to "fill my cup" and think about how I will feel when I stroll past a book store and see my novel for sale in the window. I imagine the cover illustration, my name in bold print, the title. She has encouraged me to play with these ideas. Who will surround me at my book launch party? What will it be like to see my name on the Best Seller's List? To whom will I dedicate my book? Which actor will play the lead in the movie adaptation?

For the past two years, I've committed myself to writing fiction. At times it has been lonely working from home and difficult to be self-motivated, which makes my consultations with Carla all the more important. Still, my fiction writing remains the most rewarding work I've ever done. I'm nearly finished with my first novel and my completed middle-grade book on a baseball travel team is being reviewed by an editor at a top-tier publishing house. Now, when I let my mind wander, I'm already envisioning the sequel and figuring out which teen star will be cast in the lead role...

Alice Roche Cody lives in Bernardsville, NJ, with her husband, Patrick, and their two sons. She recently completed a middle grade book about a baseball travel team and is now writing her first novel. www.alicerochecody.com

Key 4

SINGLE TASK FOR SUPERIOR RESULTS

With grace I accept my world as perfect. I release the "shoulds" and
"could haves" and gracefully enjoy the beauty of this moment. I may
be late, have forgotten something, or been angered easily. Then, I
stop. I find the grace to see the present is perfect just as it is.

Single tasking will make a huge impact on your rapid transformation. Technology has evolved at a rate far surpassing human evolution. We live in a time when multi-tasking is considered normal and even a skill to be mastered. It is a widely held belief that the more tasks you can do simultaneously, the more marketable and valuable you appear to be. From eating and e-mailing to talking while texting, listening to your kid and thinking of your to-do's, multi-tasking has no limits.

A central message of *Keyed In* is to shift away from multi-tasking. I would not ask you to quit multi-tasking entirely. This would be impossible and there are segments of the day where multi-tasking is simply a given. I am asking that you allow in the opportunities to single task. Have an intention to single task. For example, today I challenged myself to drive without speaking on my cell phone or listening to the radio. I chose to be completely aware of my surroundings. The result was that time actually passed pleasantly, and I arrived at home feeling light and refreshed.

At the nutrition school from which I graduated, The Institute for Integrative Nutrition, I was introduced to the phrase "crowd out." Crowding out refers to adding beneficial foods and water to your diet, rather than struggle to quit eating certain foods. When it comes to your daily meals, you can crowd out the cookies by adding in the pears and apples. This is an effective approach because it is gentle on the mind, and does not invite resistance.

When it comes to nutrition, crowding out does not mean you give up favorite foods. It means you consume other foods so that there is less room for those not-so-healthy food habits. Let's use the same approach to crowd out multi-tasking. Stop and think about when it is most likely that you would be able to single task. Identify projects and the time of day where single tasking is most viable for you. Experiment and add single tasking to your daily routine, just as you would those apples and pears.

Easy opportunities come up for single tasking during your day. For example, when you are brushing your teeth, engage all of your senses. Feel the brush on your teeth, smell the toothpaste, put your attention fully on the task at hand. When your mind wanders, bring it back to the feeling of your toothbrush on the grooves of your teeth.

This two minute exercise in bringing your focused attention to the present moment is a great way to build your single tasking skills. Another opportunity to single task is while washing dishes or folding laundry. In a process similar to brushing your teeth, involve your senses while washing and drying dishes. Allow the scent of the dish soap to penetrate your body and register in your brain. Feel the hot water on your hands. Let it warm your hands and arms as the temperature of the water creates an effect in your body. Notice and feel the pans and dishes you are washing. Listen to the sound your scrubbing action makes. When you do dishes in this way, you are single tasking!

Have you ever had a chat on the phone with a friend, while folding laundry? Later in the day when you encounter that neat pile of folded clothes, have you wondered how it even got done? I know this has happened to me. That's not so bad, and often a pleasant surprise when you notice the laundry done. However, what your friend shared with you on the phone call will likely be forgotten. While you were engaged in conversation, you were also engaged in folding clothes. Try sitting and having a conversation with a friend without doing anything else. You will be stunned at how much you hear!

FINDING PRESENCE

One of the great gifts in my life is my coaching work. When I am coaching clients, my intention is to be fully present and open to receiving guidance from my higher-self that will be of greatest value to my client. The act of being largely present for each one hour session is completely energizing for me. Try single tasking and see how good you can feel.

The single tasking exercises that I have recommended are really muscle building for you. When your mate or children come home and you have the chance to connect with them, try single tasking and simply listen to them. When you are eating lunch, sit—not behind the wheel of your car—and eat. Visually appreciate your food. Smell the aroma. Taste your food. Chew your food and allow digestion to begin in your mouth. Enjoy the flavors. Pause, put down your utensils, breathe, savor, chew, swallow, and repeat. To eat without reading, typing, surfing, or driving is quite a challenge. Are you up to it?

So how will single tasking benefit you? When you single task, your mind and your energy are focused upon one thing. When you focus on the matter at hand, you engage all parts of your brain, both the logical and the creative sides. You will find that tasks are completed with speed, and problems are solved more easily. An added benefit of single tasking is reduced anxiety! When you focus on what you are doing, you are not worrying about what you are *not* doing. You are not worrying about your future. When you single task, you will have energy to spare for the next task on your list.

Another idea to support your single tasking efforts is to ground yourself in the present moment. A favorite book of mine is the short parable by Spencer Johnson, MD, called *The Precious Present*. In it, you will see aspects of yourself on your journey through life. Being fully aware in the present moment is a challenge. Finding moments of presence will add great meaning to your life. A method that I use and share to get your mind, body, and spirit in the here and now is to use a touch stone. As I shared in Key 1, a touchstone is a small object that you place in your pocket or someplace where you will notice it frequently. When you feel your touchstone, which could be a smooth pebble, a sentimental charm, or small sea shell, use it as an opportunity to bring your awareness to your surroundings and what you are doing. Another fun way to get grounded in the moment is to remove your shoes and socks and have your bare feet on the floor. Press the balls and heels of your feet and each toe firmly on the ground. Feel the earth and allow the energy of the ground or floor to draw you into the present moment. Doing so will support your desire to single task.

ACTION PLAN

Choose a timer. It can be a kitchen timer, electronic timer, or a timer on your cell phone. Set it for 10-15 minutes. Identify a task or project you need to complete. Choose from examples described in this chapter, or select your own idea. Key in and ground yourself in the present moment and stay on task for the designated number of minutes.

Interfering thoughts will come into your mind. Use your senses to get back into the single-tasking moment and release the thoughts or worry that is popping up for you. If you cannot stay on task because of your interfering thoughts, keep a note pad or use an electronic device to write and release them. Be sure to stop there. Refrain from pursuing the new ideas and stay focused upon the single task at hand.

After you have completed your first conscious single tasking exercise, notice how you feel. Then, plan your next single task.

The benefits of single tasking are enhanced relationships, enhanced productivity, and, believe it or not, *more* free time.

Be open to discovering how single tasking helps you to achieve clarity, peace, and calm and ultimately contributes to transforming your life.

UNLOCKED: A TRUE STORY

When Carla originally asked me to write a section on focusing on one task at a time, I laughed. She knows me well and understands my persistent difficulty with this simple directive.

I suffer from Attention Deficit Disorder. I am not formally diagnosed; however, my son, who shares many of my characteristics, has been. My difficulty with maintaining my attention to complete even the simplest tasks is epic. I have read many books and articles on the importance of maintenance of attention and employ various tricks necessary to accomplish this mandate.

One of the most compelling arguments I have found for focus is the understanding of how the brain works. Numerous studies have arrived at the same conclusion: the brain can only fully function when it is tuned in to one task. If there is any competition for attention, the brain will not focus on either task completely.

The ability to focus on one task seems easy. However, if you actually try it, it is extremely difficult. For example, try washing dishes without talking to someone on the phone or listening to music or having numerous conversations in your head. Paying attention to the simple act of washing the dishes is really difficult. If you were to closely attend to the temperature of the water, the feel of the soap on a pan, and the clean surface of a pan, you would experience dish washing in a whole new light. You might find a new satisfaction in completing this very simple task. You might also find that you complete it faster because you give it your full attention.

My experience has been that my least productive days are the days I think I can multi-task. Some days my inability to focus leads me to repeat my mantra "stay in the room" over and over. Yesterday is a perfect example. I was exercising in the basement, when I thought of something I needed to tell my husband. Rather than writing the thought down and telling my husband later, I ran upstairs to speak with my husband. After speaking with him, I realized I needed to order Christmas cards, which I did. However, after ordering the cards, I checked a few websites. An hour after I left the basement, I realized I hadn't accomplished my task of exercising and I was running behind with all of the other things I had scheduled and I didn't really fully experience anything.

I know, deep down, I will only be satisfied with myself if I give everything to the job at hand. By the same token, I acknowledge my difficulty with sustained attention and I allow myself to concentrate on specific things for short blocks of time. For instance, as I was writing this particular piece, I was aware that I needed to come back to it several times in order to fully present my ideas. That's okay. Before I started writing I took care of several things that could have been distractions during writing. I made sure I planned out my week. I completed the dishes. I ordered some things online. I checked Facebook and e-mail. I even asked my kids not to talk to me or near me. I took care of the things that would most likely draw me away from writing.

Planning my days and weeks seems to be the biggest help in my quest for focused attention. My days often change, but as long as I have written what I would like to accomplish, I have a better chance of actually getting it done. Planning is a reality check to help me realize my limitations. The day has twenty four hours. I would love to read books all day, but I will still need to take my kids to various activities, do laundry and dishes, go food shopping and eventually sleep. The act of writing down an agenda relieves my brain from the need to keep reminding myself what I have to do. Then, when I'm doing something, I can put all of my attention on that task.

I haven't mastered the ability to focus on each task. I often fool myself into thinking I'm an amazing multi-tasker. However, I start each day new. I try to take inventory of the things that worked and the things that didn't. I prepare for the roadblocks and then accept that life is always changing. I keep in mind that I'm never going to get it all done, and it's the journey that counts!

Teresa is a stay-at-home mom who home-schools one of her children. She lives in New Jersey with her husband, two kids, two dogs, and lots of books.

Key 5

A PICTURE IS WORTH A THOUSAND TRIES

*My mind's eye is the perfect artist. I create images of exactly how
I want to feel, who I want to be, and what I want next. I use my
ability to visualize as a tool to create a life I love.*

*S*o far you have learned and practiced four keys to unlock your
inner power and transform your life. By raising your awareness to your thoughts, you can begin to claim power over what manifests in your day. Now you can trust that what you think is empowering. In doing this, worry and fear melt away. (I know you don't
want them!) Your thoughts, coupled with the high frequency of your
feelings, are integral to creating a life you love.

In Key 2 you learned to release stress using the simple yet powerful tapping technique called EFT, which was given to the world by
the generosity of Gary Craig. Your negative emotions are valid, and

they need not be labeled "bad." It is when you suppress and ignore your feelings that they begin to have power over you and may set off emotional reactivity. Both positive and negative emotions have value. Rather than stuff them, embrace them. Love and accept yourself. When you are ready to release your stress and negative emotions, use EFT. Once your stress level is reduced, you have more clarity in your thinking and are in a powerful position to manifest your desires. In the absence of stress, fear, worry, and pain, you will *respond* to challenges rather than react to them. Consider creating the habit of daily tapping, as in creating the habit of flossing your teeth. Tapping has greater benefits than flossing, and causes no pain or bleeding!

Now that you are practicing keying in to your thoughts and reducing your stress and negativity, you are on to releasing resistance and filling your own cup, as described in Key 3. When you fill your cup with what you desire to be, you make the shift from lack to abundance. Rather than focusing on what is missing in your life, you begin to notice micro-moments of what you want. As you notice and feel these experiences, visualize filling yourself up with them. This is when you become the change that you want to experience. With Key 4 you've begun what may be new to you—single tasking. Despite the urge to juggle many balls in the air, single tasking gives you the opportunity to ground yourself in the present moment. And in the present moment is your point of power. When you are present, you are in a state that is absent of fear, worry, and guilt. Who doesn't want that? It is so liberating!

PICTURE THIS

Using visualization and visual aids is the next key to unlock your personal transformation. I first learned about "creative visualization" from the book with that title by author Shakti Gawain. There are many ways to visualize and it is a natural process that you may do already. Amateur and professional athletes visualize the result that they want to accomplish. It may be the swing of their golf club as it makes contact with the ball or the landing of a powerhouse serve over the net. Using creative visualization techniques pre-pave the way for you to achieve what it is you desire. When you visualize, you create a mental picture of *you* having what you want. Notice that YOU are in the picture! It is common for people to visualize a shiny new car or a beachy vacation, but then they forget to put themselves in the picture. Including yourself in your visualization is a critical component of manifesting your desires.

I am often asked, "How can I visualize myself thin, when all I can see is my belly preceding me?" I am going to use visualizing your body transforming to its perfect shape and size to exemplify the process of creative visualization. The techniques I share will apply to visualizing your ideal romantic relationship, your abundant wealth, a fabulous career, peaceful parenting and whatever else you may dream of creating.

It is important to have a visualization strategy because "what is" will often get in the way. Key in and ask yourself, has there been a time in my life when I was thin, fit, and strong? Do I know or admire someone who has the physique I desire? If you can answer yes, then you have a basis from which to visualize. You can use your memory or imagination. You can even "cut and paste" an image of your face on another's body. Now put yourself into a scene, enjoying your ideal body. Imagine being engaged with family or friends at a location that brings you great peace and happiness. See yourself being fit and energetic, excelling in an activity (even if you don't actually excel in it currently) and feeling your best. You see yourself in your new body, and you love how you look and feel. People shower you with compliments about your vibrant fitness and health. You feel fantastic. This is an example of how to visualize what you want.

KNOW WHAT YOU WANT

When you remain focused upon what is, and what is does not feel good, you are pointing yourself away from what you truly want. Remember that all that you want already exists. You need to align your energy with receiving what you want. The work you have done so far in *Keyed In* has prepared you for allowing what you want to enter into your reality.

When you look into a mirror and see the body that you have, not the body that you imagine having, you must choose to look at yourself with new eyes. Choose to admire the beauty, strength, or flexibility that you currently have. I am not suggesting you deny the existence of that excess weight. I am asking that you express gratitude for the perfection that exists abundantly in your body already. As you practice both visualizing yourself in joyful scenes with the body you desire, and loving and appreciating the body you have in the mirror, your transformation is well on the way.

Use creative visualization to pre-pave the way for many of your daily activities. For example, before your workout, take a few moments to imagine yourself successfully completing your pushups. Visualize your strength and endurance. See yourself completing the exercises you set out to perform. When it comes to your work day, before you pick up the phone to call a prospective client, ask yourself, "How will I feel when this person says 'Yes!' to me?" Imagine yourself celebrating that success and feeling great about the work you do and the value you offer to your clients. Then stand up, breathe, smile, and dial.

If you are a student, use creative visualization to assist you on tests. What my children, clients, and I use for exams is an imaginary funnel overhead. Imagine an empty funnel open to the universe above. Know that all the answers to the impending test already exist. This is true. Someone wrote your test, and s/he has the answers. So do countless others. Now relax, breathe, and allow the answers that you need to pour into the funnel. Visualize the answers entering your mind and becoming readily accessible as you need them throughout the exam. Using this approach to test taking will boost your confidence and improve your results.

Another tool to implement the use of visualization is that of a vision board. A vision board is a physical creation using images that represent feelings, people, objects, and opportunities that you want to experience in your life. Allow yourself time to dream and imagine things you may want. They may be material things like a new home, a kitchen renovation, or a car. You may dream of having more meaningful and joyful relationships. You may want to become a mom or dad, meet your ideal mate, or learn a foreign language. There are endless people, places and things that you may want to manifest into your life. It is easy to create a vision board to boost the power of your creative visualizations.

To use a vision board to display your desires, find a cork board or foam board. Make a list to identify the people, places, things and feelings that you want more of in your life. My vision board includes images of pure water, garden-fresh vegetables, a couple working out together, a beachy family vacation, writer's resources, money, and more. Once you have your list, begin to cut and collect images and words from catalogs and magazines that arrive in your mailbox. You can also search for images on the internet and print them out. I recommend arranging these images and words in a manner that feels really good to you. They do not have to be perfect or artistic. You just have to feel positive when you see them.

Apply the clippings to your cork or foam board with a temporary application such as a tack. Using tacks on your board is helpful because you will find that the images of your desires mounted upon the board will come to fruition in your daily life. As they do, remove them and add in new desired experiences or things. Place your custom vision board in a place where you will see it and notice it on a regular basis. It is important that you do not allow your vision board to blend into the background where you no longer notice or relate to the images upon it. Move your board around from time to time to prevent it from drifting out of your awareness.

A vision board works because when you see something with your eyes, it registers in your brain through your reticular activating system. The image is locked in and your brain seeks to find similar images. Get a short hair cut, then see how many others you notice with a similar cut. These people were there before, but you were not tuned in to noticing them as you are once you have an imprint of yourself with short hair on your reticular activation system. Henriette Anne Klauser's *Write It Down, Make It Happen* is a great resource to better understand how your reticular activating system operates. Klauser's book is a favorite of mine and has a variety of techniques to support you in manifesting your dreams.

In the true story that follows, you will likely see an aspect of yourself. This client suggests how to make peace with perfectionism and accept perceived inaction as a perfect solution. She imagines her daughter's joy, she fills her cup with images of actual experiences, and she visualizes this terrific scroll of happiness that depicts her life with her daughter.

ACTION PLAN

First thing in the morning, take three quiet minutes. You can do it! Close your eyes and imagine your day unfolding exactly as you want it to. Picture your relationships, your work, your self-care, your prosperity, your safety, and more. Imagine the perfect day and be sure to put yourself into the picture. *Feel* the feelings of having what you want. This is a critical step. Your emotions are so power-ful—they have more of an impact upon your ability to manifest than your thoughts do. Emotions resonate at a frequency that make them readily line up with what you want... or don't want. So be aware! I cannot emphasize enough the importance of your keen awareness. Now that you have envisioned your day as you would like it to be, step into it with action to match and keyed in awareness. You will have an awesome day!

UNLOCKED: A TRUE STORY

I use several tactics to keep my mind from worry, anxiety, and the burden of self-imposed obligations (what I *should* do or fix or make or feel). These include meditation (breathing, mindfulness), EFT, and visualization. As a result, this practice of *truly* living in the moment causes me to be more aware of my surroundings. I'm not mentally multi-tasking any more, and as a result I feel more engaged and alive from minute to minute.

I had been hounded by guilt over family dynamics relating to my daughter. For example, when my older boys were Caroline's age, we spent long hours at the playground with friends. Caroline's afternoons, in contrast, were fallout from my "suburban-mom existence." She was either strapped in a car seat or sitting on the sidelines of someone else's sporting event.

Whereas I had been home and present, planning parties and making playdough for my two older sons, I went to work when Caroline was in Kindergarten. As a result, instead of doing the "girl" things I had always imagined, like crafting and scrapbooking and baking together, I was tired at the end of the day and would let her color alone at the table while I distractedly prepared dinner or folded laundry. Or she would watch TV. That made me feel sad and guilty because she did so alone, the boys viewing choices being inappropriate for her. And clearly I wasn't monitoring that too well or she wouldn't have just mentioned a TeenNick program. UGH! Which brings to mind my concern that she seemed to be growing up too fast. I don't want her to become one of those worldly-wise third children.

Then came the straw that broke the camel's back: Caroline's dearest friend since toddler-hood, who had become like a sister as they spent countless hours playing together, the only girls among lots of big brothers (and therefore the Band-Aid for my guilt)... she moved away.

In response to the barrage, Carla told me she thought of me as a creative person. She asked what I thought of the idea of making a collage, or some sort of art piece, to represent the fullness of Caroline's life. My response? In theory it seemed a fine idea. I couldn't imagine what I'd put on it because I couldn't see through my guilt. So Carla helped by suggested a few things. (Caroline has a beautiful smile, she spends her days in a loving school environment that I had carefully selected, etc.)

That got the wheels turning for me. I could see (in my mind's eye) the Martha Stewart-worthy piece I'd create: not only the materials I'd use (paper and oil pastels, vibrant smudgy colors, and ribbons and stickers and glitter), but the ideas I'd represent as well. Mine would be a giant piece of brown craft paper, as big as the kitchen table, covered with crayon drawings of Caroline.

I pictured her skipping and singing on the sidewalk in front of our house, with her gangly limbs flailing so freely, so childlike—I love when kids actually do these kid things, like saying "yippee." A few days later I saw Caroline in my mom's cozy kitchen, rolling cookies in powdered sugar, wearing the apron *my grandmother* made for me. That weekend she was scaling the backstop on an adjacent baseball field, instead of watching her brother's soccer game. I know everyone else thought that it was terribly dangerous. And it was! But, boy, was Caroline pleased to be towering over us all. I knew if I'd chased her she'd only have gone farther, just like when she was a toddler.

As these images came to me over time, I began to FEEL all the beauty that did exist in Caroline's world. And which I'd been too preoccupied to recognize before.

Still, days went by and I hadn't put pen to paper. Then weeks went by. Nothing. This was a familiar feeling to me: too afraid to "put it out there." Afraid that it wouldn't look good enough, that I didn't have the artistic ability, that I couldn't accurately convey the love and its beauty. This collage was just something else I couldn't do. Because I'm a perfectionist. Which can be stifling. In fact, lately I've come to realize there's no good that comes of perfectionism. Really, there's nothing that comes of it at all, at least not for me.

Then one day, a month or so later, Carla asked me how I was coming along with the collage. I struggled to come up with a responsible-sounding excuse as to why I hadn't used the technique. And I realized that my collage was ... done!

Or, more accurately, my collage is a work in progress. Although I'd never picked up a piece of paper or cropped a photo or drawn so much as a rainbow, I had been creating this masterpiece on a daily basis, through visualization.

I can't share it with anyone else, and that's ok. In fact, it's easier for me this way, because it doesn't need to be "perfect." It doesn't "need" to be anything at all. Instead, its value is in the *thinking* of it. Visualization has become a practice that I use now on a regular basis. Whenever I get nagging, guilty, what-if, coulda, shoulda, woulda feelings about Caroline, I call up my masterpiece. And as I view it, I can feel my breathing slow, my muscles un-tense and I soften into a smile. The kids probably think I'm crazy, smiling like that. But who cares?!

Sometimes, when I see Caroline do something beautiful (which happens at least once a day now that my blinders are off), I make a mental snapshot, And I visualize myself adding it to the collage, which just keeps scrolling forward full of small, treasured moments that I am so grateful to witness.

Stephanie is a Marketing Manager, creative writer, and guiding light for her beautiful family.

Key 6

AFFIRM YOUR DESIRES INTO ACTIONS

*I am open to recognizing my dream come true. It may appear
differently than I first imagined. I joyfully notice that it provides
me with the very feeling I dreamed of experiencing.*

hether the thought you dwell upon is something you desire or something you dread, the more you dwell upon it
the more likely it is to occur. Most people think of an affirmation as
a positive statement of what they intend to be, do, or have. Actually you are affirming your thoughts all day long, whether you intend
to or not. If you have a negative statement about yourself, such as "I
am not good enough," you are affirming this as well. When you are
keyed in, you will have clarity and choice and the power to affirm the
thoughts you *desire* to experience. Until then, each time you look in
the mirror and say, "I'm losing my hair" or "I've gained weight!" and

feel distaste for your physical body, you are affirming the negative. By affirming, you are asking for more of the same.

A common example of affirming what you don't want to experience is found all over the road in the form of bumper stickers. There are ribbons of many colors that are intended to raise the viewer's awareness of the cause promoted by the vehicle's driver. From my point of view, when I see "Autism Awareness" and "Breast Cancer Awareness" stickers, the words stimulate thoughts and emotional vibrations of sadness, illness, and despair. When we become aware of a condition or disease, we plunge into a state of fear or sadness. Bumper stickers would be more effective if they evoked wellness and hope. Bumper stickers that promote vibrant health, love, and caring would create a great impact since they would initiate a mass affirmation by all of their viewers. On a personal level, consider how you phrase what it is you are passionate about. Is it a statement of a "don't want" or a want? Affirming is really taking a stand, so be sure you take a stand for what you want, not for what you do not want.

PRETEND YOU'VE GOT IT

When you are keyed in and use the tools revealed in the seven steps described in this book, you *choose* to affirm what you desire to experience. In affirming, you engage with the concept of acting as if you already have what you want. A written affirmation is the positive statement of what you want to be, do, or have. You might be inclined to write it as "I want to lose twenty pounds." However, a statement of *wanting* something carries with it the energy of lack. Instead, you would phrase the idea as, "I weigh 180 pounds and feel fantastic" or whatever your goal weight is. There is a possibility you may feel emotionally out of alignment if you affirm a goal that is a stretch. If you feel this way, key in and identify what fears you have that are causing you to shrink away from your affirmation. Use the skills you have learned in Key 2 to tap away your limiting beliefs. Alternatively, you can choose a different affirmation. Rather than affirm "I weigh 180 pounds and feel fantastic," try "I am happy and healthy at my perfect weight."

I recommend you phrase your affirmations in a format I learned from philosopher Bob Proctor in the film *The Secret* by Rhonda Byrne. Begin your affirmation with "I am so happy and grateful, now that..." Your happiness and gratitude are powerful influencers in your life. When you are happy, you are expressing the joy of having what you want. Your energetic vibration is vastly different than when you are putting your attention toward the absence of what you desire. When you are grateful, you vibrate energetically at the top of the Emotional Guidance Scale, as described by Abraham-Hicks. By starting your affirmation with thoughts of happiness and gratitude, you are boosting your power to transform! When you add the words "now that" to your affirmation, you are placing yourself into the present moment, acting as if you already have what you desire. Here is an example of how to put it all together: "I am so happy and grateful now that I am earning $100,000 annually, working three days per week, and serving my clients' needs with expertise and kindness." Create your affirmation right now. Affirm areas of your life including your health, your wealth, your love life, and your relationships. Your possibilities are limitless.

Another way to affirm what you want is to do so in question form. When you ask a question, your brain automatically begins to work on finding the answer. If you ask, "How did I get ten new clients this month?" you will begin to key in to methods of growing your business while at the same time meeting those who support the growth of your business. When you are looking for a loving relationship, ask, "How did I end up meeting my soul-mate?" Your subconscious mind hears your question and works to please you by providing you with your answer.

A wonderful resource of healing affirmations is Louise Hay's classic book *You Can Heal Your Life*. Using Hay's approach, I created an affirmation to support the healing of an injury I sustained. Before a walk on a lovely summer morning, I opened my pantry and a 28-ounce can of tomatoes fell and landed on my left foot! While it startled me and hurt quite a bit, I laced up my sneakers and used EFT and tapped on the issue of the immediate pain I was experiencing. Then, I met my friend for our weekly walk without giving it much more thought. Later, using Hay's book as a guide, I came up with this affirmation: "I step forward into life and allow myself to shine." I realized that everything happens for a reason and that my injury to my foot had meaning. I chose to apply a thought process that would not allow my pain to hold me back. I would step more bravely into new situations and let the world witness my true self. Another affirmation I created is "The bones in my left foot are mending. My cells are re-generating. Healing is my choice and I allow it to happen."

I wish I could say that my foot is completely healed and is free of pain. It is not. However, what is truly amazing is that since affirming, "I step forward into life and allow myself to shine." I have written and completed this book! Like many people, I have had book ideas swirling around in my head for decades. Once I began affirming that I was *stepping forward* and *shining*, my ideas crystallized and I completed my book. Coincidence? I do not think so. I stepped into writing, took risks, revealed myself and completed the project. Now, I have shifted my approach to healing my bone. At the time when the (very large) can plummeted to the ground and landed on me, my initial feelings were anger and disgust that I was not more organized. It is my nature to rush and not take an extra few minutes to rotate groceries and put them away carefully and logically. I am inclined to just "get it done" which can be hazardous! The realization that I had unaddressed anger and disappointment in myself caused the shift in my approach. It is so important to love and accept yourself as you are, and this is how I am filling my cup. As I forgive myself for being disorganized, my toe can release the pain that reminds me I am not good enough. Affirm your well-being and allow magic into your life.

As I mentioned in Key 1, I am an admirer of author and speaker Mike Dooley. Mike sends out daily "Notes from the Universe" to his subscribers. Mike's messages are uplifting, often humorous, on target, and affirming. Recently, I was inspired by one of Mike's "notes," to create an affirmation. My affirmation is also a visualization. Here is Mike Dooley's stirring note: "You could always send a golden thought balloon to the most rocking possible version of your future self, and thank them for reaching back to you with inspiration, hunches, instincts, and impulses, to help you bridge all gaps, connect all dots, and leap tall buildings... you know, to bring about your quickest merger. Love mergers, The Universe."

I encourage you to take a moment, close your eyes, and get in touch with the wisdom that you possess and the wisdom that is available to you. Create a statement that resonates with you and produces a pathway to your higher consciousness, your expansive wisdom, and the wisdom that is available to all. I have posted on my cork board a saying similar to this: "I am sending a shiny, golden thought bubble to my future self and I thank her for reaching back to me with inspiration, and for sharing with me the truest sensation that all is well." I love the idea of my future self being a wiser, knowing being who assures me that I am on the right path. How about you?

Check in and see if you are ready to use affirmations. If you are, use sticky notes, your computer, or index cards and create positive statements in the present tense that represent your desires. Write affirmations that pertain to all areas of your life, and place them where you will see them frequently. Stand in front of a mirror and speak your affirmations out loud! Remember that you are continually affirming when you worry and have self-deprecating thoughts. Choose to get keyed in, and write down statements that represent the way you truly want to feel. If you are still resistant to using an affirmation, try affirming this: "My options multiply when my resistance lessens." You will release your resistance to using affirmations and open yourself up to endless possibilities. I love this affirmation, and it is helpful in implementing Key 3.

ACTION PLAN

I have given you plenty of examples of how and why to use affirmations. For this exercise, I want you to come up with five bumper stickers. Make this fun, funny, and a true expression of yourself.

Imagine a magnet of any shape, size, or color on the back of your car that professes what you want to see for yourself, what you want more of in your life, how you want the world to operate, and any other dream you may have. You may want to sketch it out and color it in. Go for it, and maybe you will even have them printed out and use them!

1._____

2._____

3._____

4._____

5._____

UNLOCKED: A TRUE STORY

I have worked in the financial services field for thirty years as a straight commission-based financial advisor. I have no base salary, no pension, no paid vacation and no paid time off. I have also been a single mother for the past twenty years so juggling everything between my parental responsibilities and my career has been challenging, and I have had no choice but to embrace those challenges.

About five years ago, I left a firm I had been with for fifteen years and decided upon a big move to a new firm. Shortly after I joined the new firm, it went through a major merger and restructuring which just happened to be during the height of the financial crisis of 2008-2009. Although I made an effort to maintain a positive attitude, it seemed that every aspect of my business day was requiring so much extra work, and I felt that I was working very "hard" with endless hours and never able to turn off my mind. The daily stress level was extremely high for me as well as for my coworkers. It was at that point that I contacted Carla whom I had met at a women's networking event. I was looking for any suggestions on how to continue to move forward and stay positive during the upheaval and stressful times of the financial crisis.

As a first step, Carla sent me a questionnaire to complete, and I was astounded when I answered the questions. I learned so much about myself just from her questionnaire. She pointed out that I was working very "hard" and that I should redirect my thought process to work "easier." It never occurred to me that working "easier" could even be an option since my entire life it had been ingrained in me through my upbringing that I had to work very hard to accomplish my goals.

Initially, Carla and I came up with a great affirmation which I still use daily and it specifically deals with my career desires and goals. This affirmation was the beginning of a significant transformation for me. I quickly learned that by creating very specific and detailed affirmations that my desires and goals turn into realities. Carla suggested that I type these affirmations up and place the sentences in various locations throughout my home and office and read them often. Affirmations need to be stated in the present tense. They should be positive, personal, and specific. In general, affirmations personify the practice of positive thinking and empowerment.

I believe that we are each responsible for our own experiences and every thought we think is creating our future which means that our power is in the current moment. The idea of using affirmations was the perfect suggestion from Carla for me, and it helped me prioritize and concentrate on the positives during a very difficult time.

I became very focused on visualizing what I wanted to accomplish and I began to write down my specific goals and create a very detailed annual business plan. In addition, I created a vision board with pictures, sentences and phrases that pertain to my short and long term goals and ultimate goals.

Although I still work fifty to sixty hours a week, I feel more on track with my goals and objectives, and I feel better equipped to move forward, particularly during times of challenge and adversity. In addition, I had previously been concerned about taking time off to go on vacation, but after creating an affirmation that pertains to vacations, I have been able to go away without the stress I used to feel.

One other main point that goes hand in hand with affirming desires into actions is to experience and express gratitude when things go as you had hoped and projected. I maintain a journal, and I keep track of positive experiences as well as goals and accomplishments. This is a great way for me to give thanks to the universe, and it helps me continue to move forward when negative situations or issues arise.

Jeri is a financial advisor and single mother. She incorporates positive affirmations and the concept of paying it forward in all aspects of her personal and business life.

Key 7

JAG TECHNIQUE –JOURNALING WITH POWER

*Yesterday is a powerful force behind who I am today. The
memories of my life experiences of joy, confidence, and compassion
give me the power to create what I want now in this moment. I
collect the positive feelings of yesterdays, take them with me today,
and attract what I want into my life.*

*J*ournaling is a subject that brings up a good deal of emotional
reaction when I suggest it to friends or clients. I commonly hear that there isn't enough time to keep a journal. My clients
say they wait until bed time and then are too exhausted to write,
or that they are torn between writing on an electronic device and
writing in a paper journal, so they just don't do it. I completely understand these responses, and at times I am in the same situation myself. Sometimes I imagine the next technology that will capture and

record my thoughts as I mentally journal. Journaling is not meant to feel like a "should." A should is different than a want. When you feel the weight of something to do on your shoulders, and guilt for not doing it, that is a should. Note the root of the word shoulders is should! Have you ever heard the expression "Don't should on yourself!"? Relax about journaling. You may have many valid reasons *not* to journal. Despite that, I invite you to learn about my efficient, powerful JAG process which will move your transformation along at a rapid pace.

I am going to share with you ways to make your journaling efforts easy and empowering. If you are ready to give it a try, I would like to support you in breaking through any barrier that you presently face. If you already keep a journal, my JAG technique is one that will add transformative power to your entries.

The JAG technique is something I created to help me clarify my own journaling. Because I use affirmations written as if they have already happened, I would confuse myself in my own journal! I would re-read a passage and be unclear if the event actually happened or was an affirmation. Sometimes, affirmed desires had manifested, but the date of the entry preceded the event. This is a great discovery to find in your journal, and is a true indicator of the power of writing down your intentions. At one time I kept a small notebook in my purse. Whenever the opportunity arose, I would write elaborate and lofty stories as if they had already happened. One day, I received a call from a dermatologist's office telling me they had found my notebook! I was so embarrassed that someone had flipped through my book to determine it was mine. I got over my embarrassment quickly and hoped that someone else was inspired to write their lofty life story.

Using JAG will eliminate any confusion for you and also elevate the vibrational power of your journal by packing it with gratitude.

JOURNAL

The JAG technique stands for: Journal/Affirm/Gratitude. I know it will help you. Here's how it works. Use any notebook that you have on hand, or go out and purchase something special. If you prefer, use your favorite form of technology to type your journal. To start your JAG journal, write today's date. Begin by writing the letter **J** in the margin of your journal. From there freely, without censoring yourself, begin to write, rant, and vent anything you would like about your day. Include the highs and lows and your strengths and weaknesses. You can go into detail on one aspect of your day, or you can cover it all. There are no rules. Do not feel that you have to journal about your day from morning until night in chronological order.

I addressed in the beginning of this Key that *when* you write in your journal is your decision. You have countless options. If you decide to journal before going to sleep, an advantage to you is that your JAG entries will become embedded into your subconscious mind. Your conscious awareness is just the tip of the virtual iceberg of your mind. Using JAG at bedtime will allow your words to assimilate into your being. Release any worry about whether you are doing this right, and just do it!

AFFIRM/ACT AS IF

The next step is to write the letter **A** in the margin of your journal. After the letter **A**, write your affirmations. Affirmations are statements of what you would like to experience, written in the present tense. Use the prompt "I'm so happy and grateful now that…" or use a questioning approach: "How can it be that…?" Or use both! Another way to look at the A in the acronym JAG is "Act as if." So, go ahead and write a whole story as if you are already experiencing what it is that you want to achieve. When you act as if, you go beyond an affirmation sentence and write freely as though you are experiencing, in this moment, just what you desire. State in the present tense whatever it is that you desire to be, do, or have. After the letter **A** in your margin, write a story. For example, tell about a job interview unfolding in an ideal way or about a party you are having that is a huge success! Although they may not have happened in your present moment, writing about them as if they did will expedite their manifestation.

Think about impending events on your schedule and affirm in a descriptive way your desired outcome. Release any worries about how that outcome will be achieved. When you begin to wonder about how the outcome will come about, your thoughts and feelings are infused with doubt and worry. Doubt and worry will extinguish your creative fire and deter the manifestation of your desires. Stay in the place of acting as if you already have what you want, and write on. Include a statement expressing your joy at having reached your goal.

GRATITUDE

The **G** in JAG stands for Gratitude. Gratitude is a feeling that resonates at a very high energetic vibration and will align you with the energy of having your desires. After you write the letter **G**, I suggest you write the numbers one through five in the margin of your journal, and begin to enumerate experiences from your day for which you are grateful. You can choose to be grateful for the big things, such as the fact that you woke up this morning. You can be grateful for a small act of kindness from a stranger. Possibly someone let you in front of them on a line. Keep writing until you identify four items for which you are grateful for today. The secret to boosting the vibration of your thoughts of gratitude lies in one special step. That would be item number five. Always be sure to write down something you are grateful for about yourself! Be specific. You can choose a physical aspect, an emotional aspect, or your mental ability. Find something about yourself for which you are appreciative today. This energy of love for yourself is critical in your personal transformation. When you are grateful for something about yourself, you have more to give to your loved ones because you are coming from a place of fullness. And you will feel personally fulfilled.

ACTION PLAN

Find an object you can use for your personal JAG journal. You can purchase a new journal book that fits you perfectly. You can look around your home and find a partially used notebook and begin using that as your journal. You can use your tablet or computer and start there. There is no wrong place to journal.

Determine when the best time of day will be for you to journal. Will it be first thing in the morning, last thing before going to bed, or on your lunch break? Choose a time and decide that this is when you will journal. You can also keep your journal with you and use time as it opens up for you. Your journal process can be a few minutes long, or as long as you are in the flow of writing for that particular day.

- Follow the steps outlined in this chapter.

- First write the date on your page.

- Then write the letter **J** and begin to journal freely without placing any judgments upon yourself.

- Then write the letter **A** and state the affirmations that you would like to say for the day. You can also write an "act as if" story and elaborate on your achievements in great detail.

- Last, write the letter **G**. Then write the numbers one through five as you write down the five items for which you are grateful on this day. Always include an item about yourself each and every time you write in your JAG journal.

Congratulations on adding this simple process to your life as you key in and raise your awareness to your thoughts and feelings. Journaling using the JAG process is the final key to enhance the speed and quality of your personal transformation.

UNLOCKED: A TRUE STORY

I have journaled many times in my life, but I never did it with any focus or direction. It was just a way to write about my day, often about the stress of the day so I could release it and clear my head.

Carla's approach to journaling, her JAG method, made a difference in the impact journaling had on my life. Now when I journal about my day, I have a greater awareness of my intentions as I am journaling. I may be writing about my day, including happy events or challenges, and then I use this information to leverage tomorrow and consciously create a great day.

When I journal (J), I write about the day. I express my feelings of joy or frustration with great emotion, telling all about how I felt that day. Next are my affirmations (A). When the journaling is done, then I can affirm what I see or want to see differently based on what I liked or may want to do differently tomorrow. Then it's the gratitude (G) part which I find the most rewarding. Here, I must find things to be grateful for. I generally find this easy to do, no matter how bad the day seemed when I sat down to write.

One day I was Journaling my fear and frustration because my daughter was planning to have minor elective surgery which she knew she was going to do and she had months to plan it. She waited to book the date and she called me to say that she might not come home for Christmas because it would be the only time she could do the surgery. (She needed it done by year end.) I was upset. I spoke positively to her, but when Journaling, my frustration surfaced. After expressing all my reasons to be frustrated, I needed to write my positive affirmations. I affirmed that her health was most important. I affirmed that the facility would accommodate her scheduling needs, and I affirmed that she would be home for Christmas. The next day she called to confirm she would get the surgery and be home for Christmas!

The gratitude piece was easy that day!

I write when I don't get up and exercise, don't eat right, am not as organized as I'd like, want to do more at work, want to meet/call my friends more often, anything that comes to mind. Then I can write affirmations that these things are just the way I want them to be. I thank God that I am able to accomplish my goals (as if I already have), and little by little my life has changed. Journaling allows me to take the time to focus on the everyday things that affect my life and my peace of mind. Using the JAG method, I can vent my concerns and then declare affirmations that I want to see come true. By stating what I am grateful for, I reaffirm what I already have that is working well.

I already see change happening, and I am sure that this daily acknowledgement of what I want to change is the driving force.

Andrea is a divorced mother of two girls and works as a life insurance representative. As a single mom who worked on Wall Street during the 911 tragedy and then lost her job, her life experience speaks to the benefits of living with a positive attitude and using the techniques in this book to help her through the difficult times.

KEYED IN QUIZ:

Do you want to know your *Keyed In* score? Take this test periodically and see how your keyed-in experience shifts over time. Write your answer to the left of each question. Choose from the range of numbers between zero and ten.

Score: 0 means not at all and 10 means very much.

_____ 1. How willing would you be to have your thoughts blasted out loud at the local grocery store?

_____ 2. If time was not a buffer and your thoughts manifested right before your eyes, would you be pleased?

_____ 3. What is your willingness to release stuck negative emotion from your body?

_____ 4. How likely are you to imagine the best possible outcome?

_____ 5. Are you willing to put down all the balls but one and stop juggling?

_____ 6. Like a professional athlete, do you visualize how you would like an event to unfold?

_____ 7. When someone is "driving you crazy" how willing are you to release your attention from them and look at yourself?

_____ 8. When you hear, "Be the change you wish to see" do you feel ready to release resistance and embrace a better feeling?

_____ 9. Are you willing to say, "I am good enough and, at this moment, perfect just the way I am"?

_____ 10. Will you write down your wants in a way that tells a story as if you already have your desired object, experience, or event?

_____ Total

Your Score: _____

0-20   Utilize _Key 1_ and begin to key in and choose your thoughts. You can do it!

21-40   You are building great habits. Now it's time to add in visualization.

41-60   Wow, when it comes to expecting the best and putting yourself in the picture, you have got it mastered. Just keep working on dissolving your stress so you can gain more clarity.

61-80   You are both student and teacher. Share your wisdom with those around you. Allow your bright light to shine. The world needs your voice.

81-100 Woo Hoo! You've got the keys to transformation. Welcome the new you that will be arriving very soon.

CONCLUSION

I've written *Keyed In* so you may be empowered to take hold of the wheel and steer into the direction of your dreams. Having this road map to keep you keyed in will provide structure and guidance that will culminate in your latest personal success story. Success is achieved in moments each day. Baby steps of keyed-in awareness coupled with action will make evident your desired outcome.

TO SUMMARIZE, THE 7 KEYS ARE:

1. What you think about, you bring about. Shine the light of your awareness upon your thoughts to make sure they are serving your highest interests.

2. Release stress. Use EFT (tapping) and clear out your stuck negative emotions. Make space for the new and good in your life.

3. Fill your own cup. Become the change you want to see in your life. Allow it in.

4.   Single task and your productivity will soar. Choose deliberate times or situations and put your mind to your task at hand. You will notice a tremendous difference in your energy and achievements.

5.   Visualize yourself having the experience that you desire. When you can see it happen in your mind's eye, you create the energetic pathway for it to be so.

6.   Create an affirmation. Write positive statements of what you want, as if you already have it. Have fun with this!

7.   Journal with efficiency. Use JAG and your journal will support you in experiencing your greatest moments and will tell the story of your wonderful life experience.

You are perfect just the way you are. These 7 Keys are not intended to make you feel as if you are not good enough. Each segment of the day that you incorporate even one of the 7 Keys to being keyed in will contribute to a positive experience in your life. Personally, I still need to remind myself to take each of these action steps. They are not automatic for me. (If they were, I would be on auto-pilot and would not be keyed in.) I am happy for this because each time that I visualize or tap, for example, I feel fresh and new. The 7 Keys will never feel like a boring routine. You create your story, and it is new all the time. I am so happy and grateful that you have given your time to read *Keyed In*. I feel privileged to have you be a part of my life.

Would you like to further develop the 7 Keys with me? Join my coaching club and receive support on your personal transformation. Group coaching and private coaching programs are available. Visit <u>www.keyedin.us</u> for more information.

ABOUT THE AUTHOR

Carla C. Hugo is a native New Yorker transplanted to New Jersey upon marrying her wonderful, supportive husband, Darren L. Hugo, CFP. Together they are raising two amazing teens, and growing up themselves in the process. Carla is a bit dog crazy and has three at the time. In looking back at the hundreds of articles she has written and at fifteen years of having the privilege to provide coaching to the best people on Earth, Carla decided it was time to put her work into a book. In *Keyed In* readers will find what makes her coach-approach revitalizing and transformative. This book is a reflection of Carla's personal philosophies and passions. When not working in her business, GetCoached, and lovingly supporting her family and home life, Carla's hobby is finding, preparing, sharing, and enjoying low-fat, plant-based recipes. Visit her coaching website at www.getcoached.com, her blog at www.getplantbased.com, and her book site at www.keyedin.us.

ACKNOWLEDGMENTS

I am so happy and grateful for my editor, Kimberly Flynn, who took my words as written by a life-coach (not a writer) and smoothed them out for our readers in the manner of an expert wordsmith. After each editing meeting with Kim, I left super-charged with excitement and possibilities. I had to be vulnerable to share my work with anyone, and Kim made me feel safe. The synchronicities we experienced in the process were amazing.

To the **Unlocked** contributors, I am so grateful for your trust in me. You have taken time from your busy life to write about how you have implemented the Key and have shared your results. Thank you for being vulnerable for the benefit of our readers. You are a gift to me.

To my book designer, Heather UpChurch, thank you for your creativity, flexibility and expertise. We connected randomly, yet share an uncommon common- thread.

The brainstorming for *Keyed In* began at the beach on the New Jersey shore in 2010. I knew I wanted to use a skeleton key to represent my thoughts. Thank you, Darren, for coming up with the term keyed in! I am so thankful for the family, friends, clients, teachers, and colleagues I have engaged with that have supported me in living a keyed-in life.

RESOURCES

Introduction

Splendid Life Meditation. www.splendidlifecenter.com/

Craig, Gary. Emotional Freedom Techniques. www.emofree.com/

Runkel, Hal Edward. *ScreamFree Parenting — The Revolutionary Approach to Raising Your Kids by Keeping Your Cool.* New York: Broadway Books, 2007. http://screamfree.com/

Institute for Integrative Nutrition. www.integrativenutrition.com/

Key 1

Dooley, Mike. www.tut.com

Rechtschaffen, Stephan, MD. *Time Shifting — Creating More Time To Enjoy Your Life.* New York: Doubleday, 1996. www.eomega. org/

Mardfin, Gail. www.seethegood.net

Key 2

Craig, Gary. www.emofree.com

Munn, Steven. Clear Point Center. www.clearpointcenter.com

Key 3

Jung, Carl. www.goodreads.com/quotes/search?ut-f8=%E2%9C%93&q=what+you+resist+persists&commit=-Search

Mother Teresa. www.goodreads.com/quotes/690241-i-was-once-asked-why-i-don-t-participate-in-anti-war

Key 4

Institute for Integrative Nutrition. www.integrativenutrition.com/

Johnson, Spencer, MD. *The Precious Present*. New York: Doubleday, 1984. www.spencerjohnson.com/

Key 5

Gawain, Shakti. *Creative Visualization – Use The Power Of Your Imagination To Create What You Want In Your Life*. California: New World Library, 1995. www.shaktigawain.com

Klauser, Henriette Anne. *Write it Down, Make it Happen – Knowing What You Want And Getting It*.

New York: Simon & Schuster, 2000. www.henrietteklauser.com/

Key 6

Proctor, Bob. www.bobproctorcoaching.com/

Byrne, Rhonda. *The Secret*. www.thesecret.tv/creative-biography.html

Abraham-Hicks. www.abraham-hicks.com

Hay, Louise L. *You Can Heal Your Life*. California: Hay House, Inc., 1999. www.healyourlife.com/

Dooley, Mike. www.tut.com

Photo credit: Madison L. Hugo—my gorgeous daughter with skyrocketing smarts and a flair for creativity

Notes

_____

_____

_____

_____

_____

_____

_____

_____

_____

_____

_____

_____

Made in the USA
Middletown, DE
03 May 2017